Operation
TOUSSAINT

TIM BALLARD

RUSSELL BRUNSON

NICK NANTON

NEW YORK

LONDON • NASHVILLE • MELBOURNE • VANCOUVER

OPERATION TOUSSAINT

Published in New York, New York, by Morgan James Publishing in association with Impact Publishing. Morgan James is a trademark of Morgan James, LLC. www.MorganJamesPublishing.com

ISBN 9781642792690 paperback
ISBN 9781642792713 case laminate
ISBN 9781642792690 eBook
Library of Congress Control Number: 2018910804

DNA FILMS PRESENTS
"OPERATION TOUSSAINT"
BY TIM BALLARD, RUSSELL BRUNSON & NICK NANTON

ADAPTED FROM THE DOCUMENTARY FILM.
PUBLISHED BY MORGAN JAMES PUBLISHING.

The Operations portrayed are real.

There are no reenactments.

Port-au-Prince, Haiti

"We have a story we love to talk about;

there is a young boy on a beach who is throwing starfish into the ocean. An older man approaches the young boy and says, "Boy, what are you doing?" He says, "The tide is low, the sun is high, and if I don't get them all back into the ocean they're going to shrivel up and die."

The man points to the boy and says, "Look down the beach, look down the shoreline. There's millions of them, or thousands of them. There's no way that you can get them all back. Do you think you can really make a difference?"

The young boy thinks for a moment, and then just starts tossing starfish back into the ocean. He turns to the older gentleman and says, "I don't know, but I know I just made a difference for that one."

48 hours earlier

Salt Lake City
Utah

Utah Attorney General
Sean Reyes

SCENE/LOCATION:
Conference in Salt Lake City, Utah

SEAN REYES
Utah Attorney General:

Thank you very much ladies and gentleman. Thank you. Thank you. Good morning. It's great to see this many of you out. Thank you, each and every one of you who came out today to support Utah's efforts in the fight against this horrible, evil institution that we call human trafficking. There are over 40 million modern day slaves worldwide, and thousands of them throughout the United States. Many of you have known about this issue, and have been fighting against it and working here for years, some even decades.

This is an institution that's been around since the beginning of time, but it's really only now that the mainstream, the public, is starting to gain awareness. A little over four years ago, a dear friend of mine who was a superstar in the law enforcement community—he was a specialized agent with a very special set of skills—left his law enforcement career and everything that he knew, his pension and his security, to start a nonprofit called Operation Underground Railroad.

They've done jumps everywhere throughout the world. They've rescued kids, and then helped them get to safe places with their aftercare programs. Tim Ballard, are you here? Can you come on up, so we can recognize you and Operation Underground Railroad.

TIM BALLARD
Former Special Agent, Homeland Security / Child Sex Tourism Jump Team:

I'll be very brief. To invoke history, in 1791, the Haitian population rose up and destroyed slavery in their country, which was led by Toussaint Louverture. The abolitionists in America were watching. Fredrick Douglas was watching, and he used that inspiration. When slavery was finally eradicated legally—because it has not been eradicated in actuality—Fredrick Douglas said, "Let us not forget the sons and daughters of Haiti, who are the true pioneer abolitionists of the 19th century."

We'll turn the rest over to God, and pray for us all as we take our flights in the next 24-48 hours, and execute this operation. I am certain we will have success. Thank you so much.

"Let us not
forget the sons
and daughters of
Haiti, who are
the true pioneer
abolitionists of
the 19th century."

Fredrick Douglas

DIMITRI: "We've identified almost four traffickers. We're just waiting for your word."

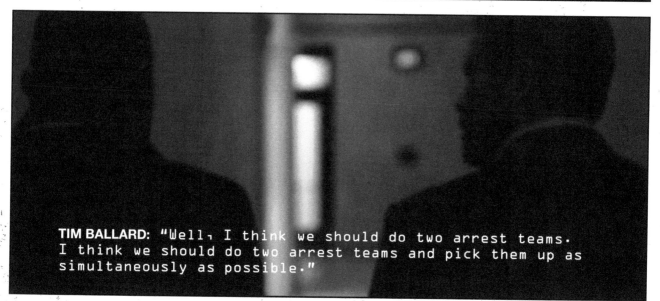

TIM BALLARD: "Well, I think we should do two arrest teams. I think we should do two arrest teams and pick them up as simultaneously as possible."

DIMITRI: "Yes sir. We absolutely are going to need your assistance on this."

Haitian Attorney General
Clame Ocnam Dames

SCENE/LOCATION:
Operation Toussiant Briefing

SEAN REYES:

Well, ladies and gentleman welcome. We're here to discuss preparations for what we are so excited for. It's a day that we've waited a long time for, and we want to thank my colleague, Attorney General Ocnam [the Haitian Attorney General], who's here with his team. Then, our friends at the DCPG, the judicial police for Haiti.

Our philosophy is, it doesn't matter what country the kids belong to or were born in, they're all our kids and we want to protect all of them. But, sometimes people in our own country ask us, "Why are you going to Haiti? Why does O.U.R, or why would the Attorney General spend time in another country? We need you here."

Our response is, "On global crimes, like human trafficking, we can't pretend that it just happens in the United States. We work on it here domestically, so that we can protect our friends and allies, and also protect ourselves so it never comes into the United States borders."

TIM BALLARD:

The US creates the demand. The highest, the highest producer and consumer of child pornography is right here in the United States. So we know that it's our countrymen that are causing this. Because, we look like those evil countrymen of ours, we can get access quickly to the dark, to the evil. So the police asked,

"Do you have operators who can go undercover, into the belly of the beast, into the darkest places and find these kids?" I said, "Yes, we do."

SCENE/LOCATION:
Interview with Tim Ballard,
Former Special Agent, Homeland
Security / Child Sex Tourism
Jump Team

ADDITIONAL DETAILS:
Ballard, recalling past Operation
Voo Doo Doll, 2014

TIM BALLARD:

Something happened to me once. This was after I had quit the government, and I was already with Operation Underground Railroad. I was about to go into this compound in Port-au-Prince, Haiti. It was a trafficking center, but it looked like an orphanage from the outside; it had orphanage written on the wall. The police asked us to go in undercover, like we were going to go buy kids.

I remember sitting outside the gate; and I always fight with this. See, the problem with me is, I have seven kids. So, any kid that we're looking to save, the minute I see that kid, I think, "Oh he's six, I've got a six year old. Oh he's 10, I've got a 10 year old." It's so easy for my mind just to, basically, super impose my kid's face, my child's face, on this victim's face. I fight it, and I fight it, and I fight it. That's how I would move on, but those first couple experiences…it just almost destroyed me.

As I was standing outside the orphanage something happened, I looked in and I saw 28 kids, and that was more than I had ever seen. And, it happened again, "Oh my gosh, there's Blain, there's Jimmy, there's Sam…all my kids are here."

I remember being outside that place, and I thought I'm not going [to be able] to do it. I'm going to [have to] embrace this. I've got to buy a kid. These people think we're here to buy kids, and they made it very clear within the first five minutes. They said, "You know we don't adopt kids, right? You know we sell kids?"

I'm like, "Oh of course. Yeah, that's why we're here."

I see this little boy walk around from this dark out building. He walks into the yard of this, this dirty place. It's stinky. It smells like urine, and feces, and it was just horrible. I went up to this kid, and I picked him up. He was my kid. You know, I saw my kid, and he became my kid. So I'm holding him, and my partner is negotiating with the bad guys about the price.

They're saying, "Oh, I think you guys want that one. Okay."

These horrible people are telling us tips on how to evade the police, how they've done this before, and how to get them out of the country.

So, I pick the kid up and I want to go into the dark, kind of out buildings that are around this compound, but I don't want to look like I'm being overly

MISSION NAME	OBJECTIVE	STATUS
Operation Toussaint	Operation Underground Railroad and the Fight to End Modern Day Slavery	Ongoing

Former Special Agent
Homeland Security /
Child Sex Tourism Jump Team
Tim Ballard

FILE NO. 19

curious. I have kids, so I know how to communicate with kids. I get [the child] to point in the room, as if he's going to show me something. I look over at the bad guys, and I can tell they're like, "Oh, he wants to show that guy whatever." So it worked.

I got in there, and it just got stinkier and darker. I walk into the belly of this dark building; it got quieter and quieter as I got further away from the sounds of the street and the other kids playing outside. The quieter it got, the better I was able to hear what was always there, right behind me. It was the footsteps of this little child who was following me. I flip around and there's this little girl, and she's looking at me. I don't want to cause more tension, so I give her a candy bar.

Now again, these kids are starving. She takes that candy bar, and she looks at me, and then she looks right back at the little boy in my arms. Without taking her eyes off him, she breaks it in half, like muscle memory, and gives it to him. I'm just thinking, "This is not normal." Then it hit me, "Oh my gosh, they're brother and sister." She's horrified, because how many Westerners have been here and picked up a child, and that child disappeared and was never seen again?

"This is all she has. The only adults in her life were trying to sell her."

Operation Voo Doo Doll

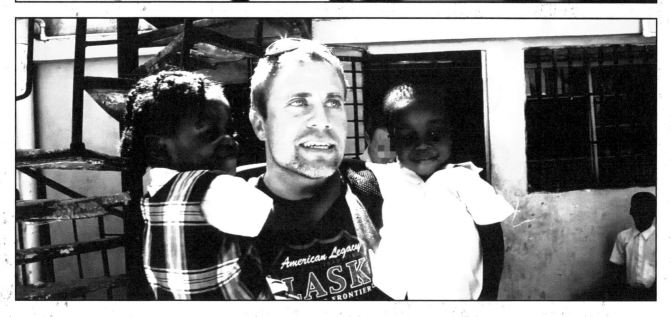

ADDITIONAL DETAILS:
Dialogue from Operation Voo Doo Doll in 2014

TIM BALLARD:
How old is she?

HAITIAN WOMAN:
Nine.

TIM BALLARD:
Nine? You're nine? How long has she been here? How long has she been here?

HAITIAN WOMAN:
 Four years.

TIM BALLARD:
Four years.

SCENE/LOCATION:
Interview with Tim Ballard, continues.

TIM BALLARD:

Every 30 seconds a child is sold. They're sold for sex, they're sold for labor, they're sold for organ harvesting, which is something we're now getting into. There are six million children that are forced into one of those three categories right now.

ADDITIONAL DETAILS:
Quote taken from Tim Ballard interview

"Modern day slavery really is the plague of our generation. When you consider there's more people enslaved today then ever before in the history of the world, and the world doesn't know. We need to wake them up."

TCR 21:32

PLAY

These girls are gonna
get naked...right away.

TCR 27:28

PLAY

If any of the girls don't perform

TCR 29:40

PLAY

You call him, he'll go and they'll
be like...firing squad.

EXECUTIVE PRODUCERS
RUSSELL BRUNSON
TODD DICKERSON

PLAY   LOCK

TCR 00:05:17:25

EXECUTIVE PRODUCERS
JW DICKS
NICK NANTON

PLAY   LOCK

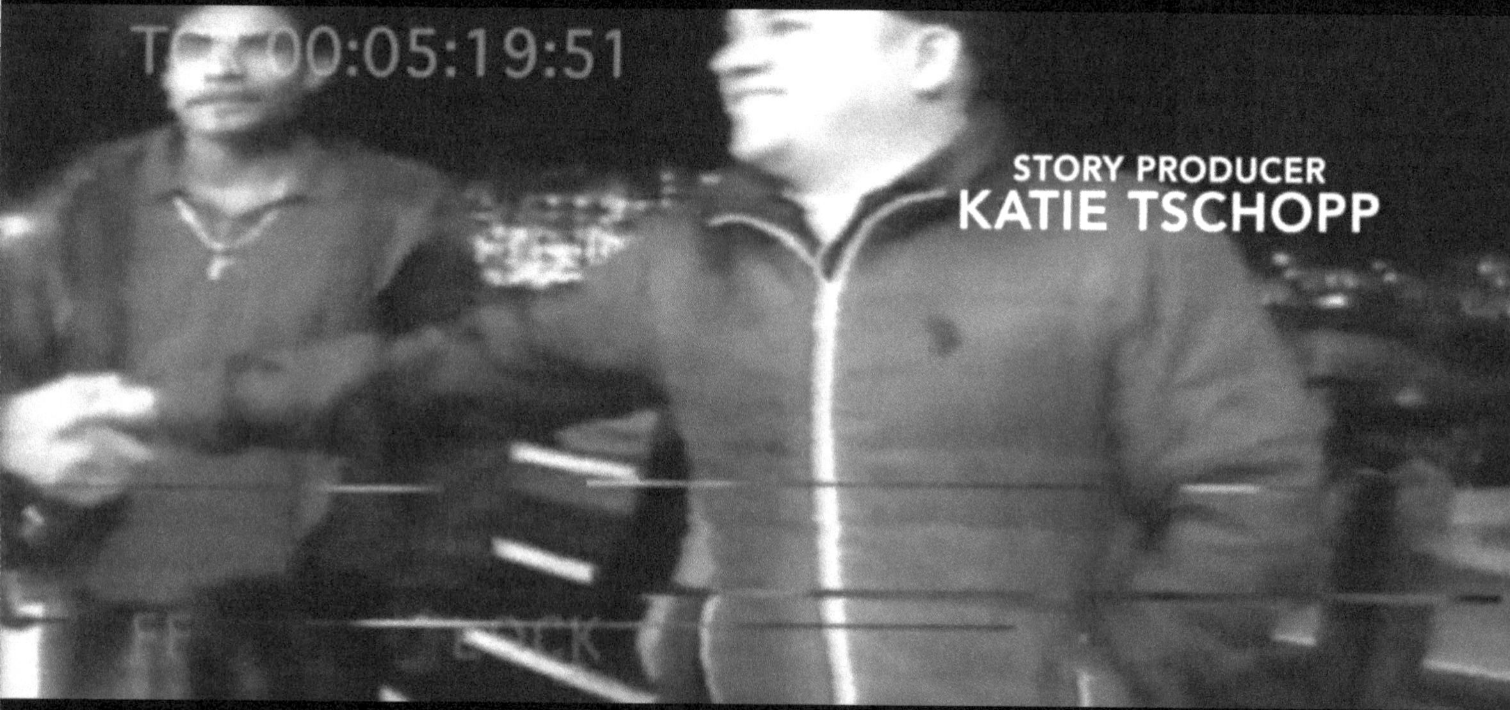
00:05:19:51
STORY PRODUCER
KATIE TSCHOPP

DIRECTOR OF PHOTOGRAPHY
RAMY ROMANY

TCR 00:05:25:10

ADDITIONAL CINEMATOGRAPHY BY
CARLO ORECCHIA
SHAWN VELA
MARK MABRY

TCR 00:05

ADDITIONAL CINEMATOGRAPHY BY
JACOB JUSTICE
JAKE CHRISTENSEN
DAVE TUCKER

PLAY

TCR 00:05:37:11

EDITED BY
NICK RUFF

PLAY   LOCK

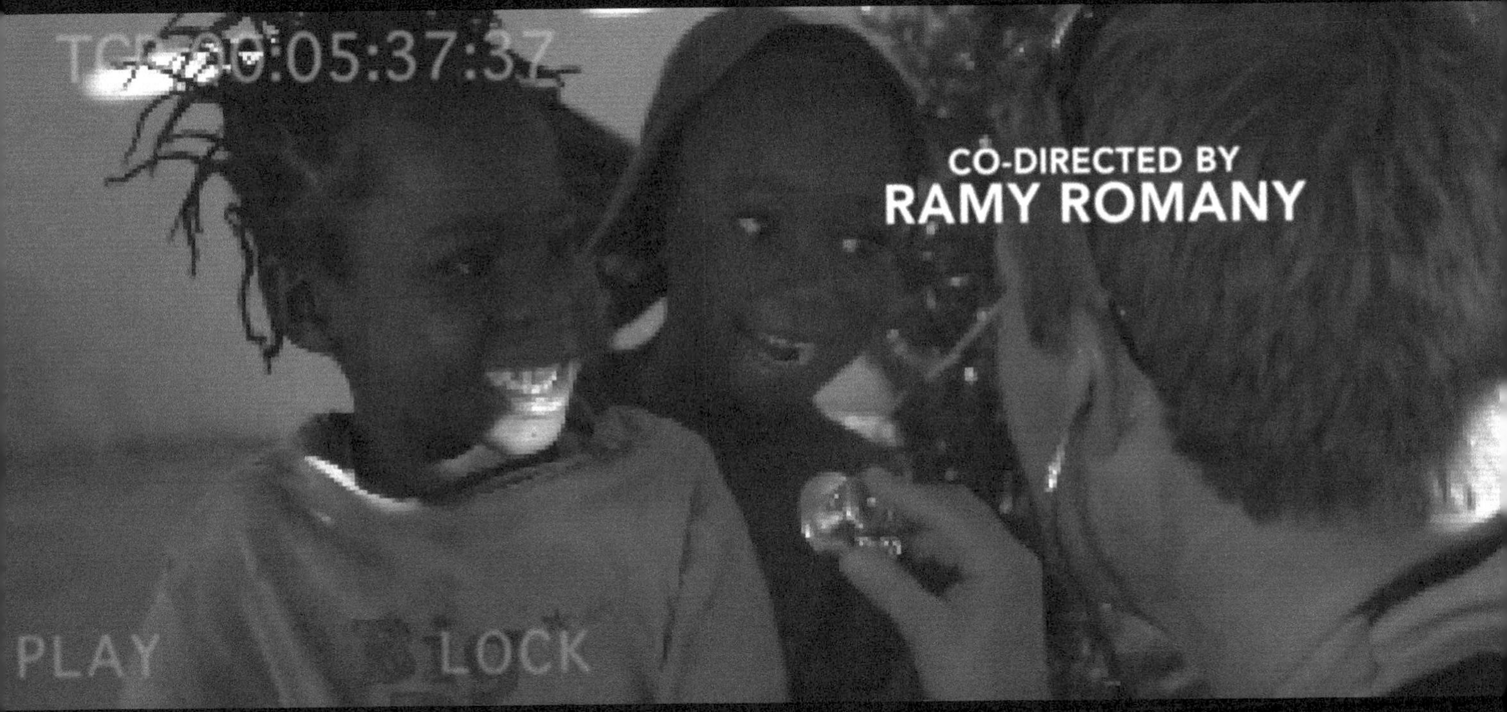
TCR 00:05:37:37
CO-DIRECTED BY
RAMY ROMANY
PLAY
LOCK

TCR 00:05:39:36

DIRECTED BY
NICK NANTON

PLAY   LOCK

Operation
TOUSSAINT

SCENE/LOCATION:
Interview with Tony Robbins

TONY ROBBINS
Life Coach/ Entrepreneur and O.U.R. Ambassador:

It's a subject that nobody wants to think about or talk about. That's part of the problem, right? It's so ugly. It's the worst part of humanity, and yet you've got to do something about it. It's kind of a catch 22: Nobody wants to talk about it. Nobody wants it to happen. Nobody wants to talk about it. Nobody wants to do anything about it.

Tony Robbins
Life Coach / Entrepreneur
O.U.R. Ambassador

SCENE/LOCATION:
Interview with Glenn Beck

GLENN BECK
Entrepreneur and O.U.R. Ambassador:

Everybody…it just drives me crazy how everybody is arguing that they would be the biggest abolitionists, [if they were] back in time. Well, would you? Because you're not doing it now. And it's not that you wouldn't, you just won't look at it.

Mike Tomlin
Pittsburgh Steelers Head Coach
O.U.R. Ambassador

SCENE/LOCATION:
Interview with Mike Tomlin

MIKE TOMLIN
Pittsburgh Steelers Head Coach and O.U.R. Ambassador:

Because I imagine a lot of people are like, "Oh yeah that's good. Man, that's awesome work they're doing." But they really...sit down, man. Like sit down, sit still for 10 minutes. You know? Really look at it. If you did that....

SCENE/LOCATION:
Interview with Marisol Nichols

MARISOL NICHOLS
Actor and O.U.R. Ambassador:

It rocked me to my core. To think about, in this day and age, people, adults and children, are being held against their will and sold by the hour to strangers to get raped; and this is their life.

Marisol Nichols
Actor
O.U.R. Ambassador

SCENE/LOCATION:
Interview with Tim Ballard, continues

TIM BALLARD:

People ask me, "Who are these dirt bags? Who are these people?" I have to tell them, "It's anybody." Anyone you can imagine. Anyone you see on the streets. It's professionals, doctors, lawyers...

SCENE:
News Clips

NEWSCASTER:
It's judgment day for former MSU Doctor Larry Nassar
for sexually abusing gymnasts under his care.

JUDGE JANICE CUNNINGHAM:
You are a doctor. You took an oath to do no harm,
and you have harmed over 256 women. And that is
beyond comprehension.

NEWSCASTER 2:
The judge also said, Nassar was able to get away
with his criminal sexual conduct for 25 years.

40-125 YEARS BEHIND BARS

@WXYZ DETROIT | JUDGE SENTENCES LARRY NASSAR TO 40-125 YEARS PUNISHMENT FOR SEX CRIMES IN EATON COUNTY

SCENE/LOCATION: Interview with Tim Ballard, continues

TIM BALLARD:

Here's the thing that's mind-boggling. It's estimated that there are over two million children, I'm not even talking about the adults, two million children currently forced to be sex slaves; raped for money. Two million. What kind of demand—and this is a scary question—what kind of demand justifies that number? Two million kids. That's a lot of sick, twisted pedophiles.

SCENE/LOCATION:
Clips from news are shown

NEWSCASTER 3:

Jared Fogle arrived here at the federal courthouse this morning. He had nothing to say. He is pleading guilty to conspiracy for receiving and distributing child pornography, and also traveling out of state to engage in commercial sex acts with minors.

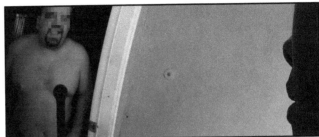

SCENE/LOCATION: Interview with Tim Ballard, continues

TIM BALLARD:

These guys want 10 year olds, 11 year olds. That's who they want. The answer to this question is not popular. People don't want me to say it; they don't want to talk about it. But, what is happening in this country, especially in this country…the United States is the highest consumer of child pornography, or what I call child rape videos, because that's what they are.

"It's the western world… The highest consumers, it's us."

SCENE/LOCATION:
Clips from Police Raid

DEPUTY:

Sheriff's office, we have a search warrant.

CRIMINAL:

I'm getting pants.

DEPUTY:

We're here to talk to you about your computer.

SCENE/LOCATION:
Interview with Tim Ballard, continues

TIM BALLARD:

And this is why. They're sex addicts. Their minds are twisted and sick to want this. I've interrogated dozens and dozens and dozens of these guys over the last 16 years that I've been working in this field.

No one wants to accept what it is. They don't want to believe it.

How did you get here? Why do you want this? Why do you want kids? And they all have the same story... "I picked up a Playboy Magazine when I was 12 years old, and then I got into more hardcore, and then more hardcore. Then the Internet came along in my 30s. Oh my gosh, I could, with a click of the mouse, I could see anything I wanted. Then the stuff that I had enjoyed since I was a teenager started to wear off. I wasn't getting the fix; I wasn't getting the feeling that I used to get when I was just watching an adult man and an adult woman have sex. Barely legal."

That's when they start searching into the queue, to the Google stream. Well that's not doing it for them anymore.

[They say,] "Okay 16, I'm going to stop there. I'm going to stop at 16, see what happens."

All of a sudden they're at 10, they're at nine, they're at eight, they're at seven. Do you think you can find this stuff online? Absolutely, and that's what's creating this demand. That's why Johns get on an airplane and fly to Haiti, Columbia, and Thailand, because pretty soon the child porn isn't doing it for them, and they need the child. This is why there's two million children forced into the commercial sex trade today.

SCENE/LOCATION:
Operation Toussiant Briefing

SEAN REYES:

People weren't talking human trafficking like they are now, and really it's because of the work and efforts by organizations like Operation Underground Railroad. He will never talk about himself, but Tim is a well respected author, lecturer, professor, and he could have a quiet life doing that. Kind of like Indiana Jones, he has another side to him and that's his law enforcement career.

He was a respected law enforcement agent for many years. Because his heart is so big, and he's so compassionate and wants to protect every child, man, and woman that he possibly can in the world, he left the comfort of his badge, his pension, and his way of life in law enforcement several years ago to step out with a lot of faith and create Operation Underground Railroad. At the time he and Katherine (Tim's wife) did it, they had no promise that anybody was going to care.

SCENE/LOCATION:
Interview with Jonathan Lines

JONATHAN LINES
Tim's Former Commanding Officer, Homeland Security:

You don't just jump on a plane and traipse into a country, and say, "Here I am, where can I go save somebody." There are so many things that have to be considered. You're shedding your badge, you're shedding your firearm, you're shedding your authority, you're shedding all the jurisdictional limitations that prohibit people from doing that very thing. But, Tim had the courage to do that.

Jonathan Lines
Tim's Former Commanding Officer
Homeland Security

Jerry Gowen
Chief Operating Officer
Operation Underground Railroad

SCENE/LOCATION:
Interview with Jerry Gowen

JERRY GOWEN
Chief Operating Office, Operation Underground Railroad:

I think there's something to say about Tim's persistence;
I guess is the word I would use for him. He wants to be a
consistent influence in your life and he's dedicated, and I
noticed those same things as he got into government work.
That he wanted to get in and make a difference, and shake
things up. You could tell he wanted to get in there and make
something happen.

CIA Headquarters

SCENE/LOCATION:
Interview with Tim Ballard

TIM BALLARD:

I grew up in Southern California. I always knew that I wanted to be a federal agent. I just wanted to do that. I don't know why, it was just inherent. My family wasn't excited about it. My parents thought it was crazy. No one in our family had been military, even generations back, or law enforcement. But it was something that I just wanted to do. So I pursued it in everything I studied. I studied political science and I studied international relations.

My first job after graduate school was at the CIA. I worked in the operations center. My study had been around terrorism and weapons. I graduated from graduate school in December of 2001. So the government was wide open for terrorist experts, and that's what I wanted to do.

As I was learning about what happened at 9/11, I learned that one of the terrorists had come from Mexicali, Mexico and came through the port of entry into California. From there [he went] back east, and then helped launch those attacks. I wanted to get on a border. I spoke Spanish, I thought I wanted to help investigate and defend against terrorist, potential terrorists that would hurt our country. I got the office in Calexico, California. I had my dream job. I mean, I was sitting on the border. My office was on the border. I could see the Mexican flag waving outside my window.

This was the time when we were finding a bunch of tunnels through San Diego, and all the way through the border on California. I was crawling through tunnels, and we were...It was great, but it only lasted for about six months. I was called in by my boss, and he told me that we were starting a new anti-child trafficking group.

SCENE/LOCATION:
Interview with Jonathan Lines, continues

JONATHAN LINES:

We knew that bad people were transmitting and receiving exploitive information, very, very dangerous information, and they were violating children. Literally, real time, and were exchanging those imageries and videos on camera with their cohorts around the world. We realized how absolutely pervasive the problem of child exploitation was.

$500 for 4 hours.

Katherine Ballard
Founder, Child Liberation
Tim's Wife

SCENE/LOCATION:
Interview with Kathering Ballard

KATHERINE BALLARD
Founder, Child Liberation, Tim's wife:

A supervisor contacted him and said, "Hey, we're thinking about starting a child's crime group, and we want you to do it." He came home and told me about it, and we were both like, "There is no way that we will ever do that." We had two little kids at the time. It just sounds so horrific. We didn't think that that was something we wanted to bring into our home.

My husband just has this light. He's able to see good in the world. You know? And he has a lot of optimism, a lot of strength. I didn't want to see that taken away. I didn't. We were raising a young family, I didn't want to see that gone. So we took it very seriously.

SCENE/LOCATION:
Interview with Tim Ballard, continues

TIM BALLARD:

My wife and I had vowed that the one thing I wouldn't do was child crimes. So we said no. I remember going home that night to my wife and saying, "You won't believe what they just asked me to do." She said, "Well you're not doing it." I said, "I'm not doing it. Absolutely not." She said, "We have kids. You can't do it."

I remember a sleepless night, that night, and then getting up the next morning and kind of looking myself in the mirror, practicing my rejection talk. As I was preparing my speech, my wife came up to me emotional with tears in her eyes. She said, "We're making a huge mistake." She said, "The very reason I thought we couldn't do this, or shouldn't do this, is the reason we need to do this, because we have kids. Because we know what childhood is supposed to be. And if it's true that there are millions of kids that are forced into that hell, how do we say no? Because we're afraid of our own pain, which is nothing relative to that pain?"

SCENE/LOCATION:
Interview with Kathrine Ballard, continues

KATHRINE BALLARD:

But I told him that I had automatic veto power. That if I ever saw anything in him—just the dimming of the lights or anything—that I got to automatically pull the plug; no questions asked and he would leave that group.

SCENE/LOCATION:
Interview with Tim Ballard, continues

TIM BALLARD:

So I reluctantly went and changed my speech, it was just one word, "Yes," and we got into it. Then something happened that was completely transformative for me. We were doing these child pornography investigations, and one of the kids from the video surfaced, and happened to surface right on the border where I was working.

SCENE:
News Story Clips

NEWSCASTER:

Not long ago, a horrific video of a five-year-old
boy being sexually abused in the worst way was
discovered by the US authorities. The boy and his
12 year old sister, they had been kidnapped, and
they had been trafficked back and forth between
the US and Mexico.

GLENN BECK:

Both were sex slaves to a monster of a man. Well
something happened. Divine providence stepped in.
It took place at the US/Mexico border. The boy
was seen by a US official who knew who he was and
identified [him as] the boy in the video.

OPERATIONUNDERGROUNDRAILROAD.ORG

SCENE/LOCATION:
Interview with Tim Ballard, continues

TIM BALLARD:

It was the first time that I was actually seeing one of the kids from the videos. It was an American man who lived in the LA area. He had a big warehouse and inside his warehouse was a house, like a residential home. Inside that home there were cameras, hidden cameras everywhere, porn everywhere, toys everywhere. He'd bring these kids in to desensitize them, and he'd make child rape videos.

As the dust settled in the investigation this kid ran to me. I remember, he jumped into my arms and just held me, and he was shaking. He just said to me with tears in his eyes, holding me and shaking, he said, "I don't belong here." I came home and I walked through the door, and I saw my kids running around playing. I couldn't handle the dichotomy.

My brain couldn't handle it, and I shut down. I mean, this is embarrassing, but this is what happened:

I remember my knees gave out as I sat there. The room was spinning and I collapsed. I fell down on the floor, and my wife thought I was having a heart attack or something. She ran over to me, and just wrapped her arms around me, and just held me.

SCENE/LOCATION:
Interview with Jonathan Lines, continues

JONATHAN LINES:

I had a knock on my door one day. Of course, I usually keep my door open, but I think I was on a phone call so I didn't answer the door immediately. But, I went to the door, and I saw Tim leaving. I said, "Hey Tim, I'm done. Come on in."

He was very, very concerned. I could tell he was perplexed. I could tell he was emotionally drained. I could tell that needed someone to talk to. He said, "Listen, I really feel like I could do better, leaving the government."

MISSION NAME	OBJECTIVE	STATUS
Operation Toussaint	Operation Underground Railroad and the Fight to End Modern Day Slavery	Ongoing

SCENE/LOCATION:
Washington D.C.

THE HONORABLE ORRIN G. HATCH
U.S. Senator, Utah:

Well, if you lost one of your children to these evil people, you'd do anything to get even and get your child back, which some of our folks are trying to do.

SCENE/LOCATION:
Tim Ballard at a Congressional Meeting

TIM BALLARD:

Good afternoon Mr. Chair and esteemed members of the committee. Thank you very much for this opportunity. My name is Tim Ballard, I'm the founder and CEO of Operation Underground Railroad.

SCENE/LOCATION:
The Honorable Orrin G. Hatch's Office

THE HONORABLE ORRIN G. HATCH:

You know, I think our own law enforcement in this country needs to get more involved than they are right now.

SCENE/LOCATION:
Tim Ballard at a Congressional Meeting

"In 2006 with the passage of the Adam Walsh PROTECT Act, Congress opened the doors for US agents to better investigate these cases, especially internationally."

CASE NAME	OBJECTIVE	STATUS
Operation Toussaint	Operation Underground Railroad and the Fight to End Modern Day Slavery	Ongoing

SCENE/LOCATION:
The Honorable Orrin G. Hatch's
Office

THE HONORABLE ORRIN G. HATCH:

It's hard because a lot of this is off shore where they may not have jurisdiction.

SCENE/LOCATION: Tim Ballard at a
Congressional Meeting

TIM BALLARD:

However, I often felt helpless by the fact that the vast majority of the child victims we would find fell outside the purview of the United States.

SCENE/LOCATION:
The Honorable Mia B. Love's
Office

THE HONORABLE MIA B. LOVE
U.S House Representative, Utah:

"It's very difficult
because we, in the
United States, have
a lot of protections
for privacy,
especially when it
comes to financial
transactions. But,
how do we get the
information to see
a pattern of sex
trafficking?"

SCENE/LOCATION: Interview with Tim Ballard, continues

TIM BALLARD:

Before this law [the Adam Walsh PROTECT Act] was passed, it was passed in 2006, in order to prosecute an American who was sexually abusing children in other countries, on the US side, you had to prove that that person had intent to rape that child while standing on US soil. So, you can imagine how many prosecutions we had prior to this law; like zero.

SCENE/LOCATION: Tim Ballard at a Congressional Meeting

TIM BALLARD:

Unless I could tie a US traveler to the case, I would not be able to rescue the children, even the ones that we were able to identify as being victims. It's outside of the jurisdiction, and I understood that, however that doesn't mean that we couldn't be doing more.

SCENE/LOCATION: The Honorable Orrin G. Hatch's Office

THE HONORABLE ORRIN G. HATCH:

It takes a little bit of an effort, but that's what we've got to do. We've got to fight like hell to try and get these kids back, and get them back on track. But in a lot of cases, once they're gone, they're gone.

SCENE/LOCATION:
Conversation between Glenn Beck and Tim Ballard. Dallas, Texas

GLENN BECK:

We need to find some partners that are like-minded. Is there a way that we can help each other?

TIM BALLARD:

Yeah

GLENN BECK:

Cause we're in the same kind of business. You know, who has big, big lists that we can leverage me? And say we'll help you, you help us.

TIM BALLARD:

Have you ever connected with... (audio fades out)

SCENE/LOCATION:
Interview with Glenn Beck, continues

GLENN BECK:

I met Tim through, I think, a series of coincidences that lead me to one of his books. He's a tremendous writer and a tremendous researcher. I mean he's really bright. So I knew him as an author and we became friends, and I didn't know that he had this secret double life.

I was coming in, I don't remember where it was, but I was coming into town and he was in town. And he said, "Hey, do you mind if we meet and talk?"

I said, "Sure. I'm going to be staying in the hotel, this hotel. Why don't you just come up?"

And he said, "Well, I, why don't we meet in a conference room?" Okay.

SCENE/LOCATION:
Tim in the Conference Room with Glenn Beck and other attendees explaining O.U.R.

TIM BALLARD:

"I'm wanting the world to wake up to what's going on; two million children are sex slaves."

SCENE/LOCATION:
Interview with Glenn Beck, continues

GLENN BECK:

He reached under his shirt and he pulled a federal badge out. On the chain it sat there. I looked at everybody and said, "Am I in trouble? Am I going to prison? What is this?"

SCENE/LOCATION: Tim in the Conference Room with Glenn Beck and other attendees explaining O.U.R.

TIM BALLARD:

It's the fastest growing criminal enterprise in the world. I go back to 19th Century America, to the slave problem. We congratulate ourselves: We got rid of, we eradicated, slavery. It's bull crap. We've not eradicated it.

SCENE/LOCATION:
Interview with Glenn Beck, continues

GLENN BECK:

He explained what he was doing and explained that he needed to get out of working with the government and he had a way that he could really make an impact, but they needed a million dollars to start it.

SCENE/LOCATION: Tim in the Conference Room with Glenn Beck and other attendees explaining O.U.R.

MEETING ATTENDEE:

It's $10,000 to put a jump team together and go, if it's overseas, I'm assuming?

TIM BALLARD:

Yeah, we have jump teams that do this. They're ex-Navy Seals, they're ex-people like me that are willing to do this.

SCENE/LOCATION: Interview with Glenn Beck, continues

GLENN BECK:

I happened to be with an attorney, he was sitting with me and I asked a whole bunch of questions and my attorney said, "No, you can't. You can't. What happens if something goes wrong? Blah blah blah. If you're raising money and it's on the border, and these guys are...You're in Texas."

SCENE/LOCATION: Tim in the Conference Room with Glenn Beck and other attendees explaining O.U.R.

MEETING ATTENDEE:

"Glenn, aren't you going [to be] surveilling and spying on people? Isn't that what this is? That people are using the Internet in the privacy of their own home. I'm not condoning the action, I'm just saying that..."

GLENN BECK:

"Child pornography? You're damn right I would. I would do it through law enforcement and I would do it exactly legal, but, I mean, this is child trafficking."

SCENE/LOCATION: Interview with Glenn Beck, continues

GLENN BECK:

Tim is the most sincere, most honest, honorable man I think I've ever met. And I said, "I'm in. We'll raise your first million."

SCENE/LOCATION: Tim in the Conference Room with Glenn Beck and other attendees explaining O.U.R.

GLENN BECK:

We're not saying we become a police force.

MEETING ATTENDEE:

No, no. I'm just worried that they bust down the wrong door and you know...

GLENN BECK:

Bring it on! I will promote, I will do. I will... I will work with you. My time, my network. Everything is at your disposal.

SCENE/LOCATION: Interview with Glenn Beck, continues

GLENN BECK:

I had a great, great, great uncle and I had a great, great grandfather who both died in the notorious concentration camp in the South. They were fighting for the North. I didn't know that. Nobody in my family knew that. They were fighting to free the slaves...

"They did it. Why can't I?"

MEETING ATTENDEE: It's $10,000 to put a jump team together and go, if it's overseas, I'm assuming?

TIM BALLARD: Yeah, we have jump teams that do this. They're ex-Navy Seals, they're ex-people like me that are willing to do this.

MEETING ATTENDEE: Glenn, aren't you going... surveilling and spying on people? Isn't that what this is? That people are using the Internet in the privacy of their own home. I'm not condoning the action, I'm just saying that...

GLENN BECK: Child pornography? You're damn right I would. I would do it through law enforcement and I would do it exactly legal, but, I mean, this is child trafficking.

GLENN BECK: We're not saying we become a police force.
MEETING ATTENDEE: No, no. I'm just worried that they bust down the wrong door and you know...

GLENN BECK: Bring it on! I will promote, I will do. I will... I will work with you. My time, my network. Everything is at your disposal.

TIM BALLARD:

"You know, Abraham Lincoln, when he was grappling with the Emancipation Proclamation, the nation didn't want him to do it. Even in the North, they didn't want him to do it. He went through something. In 1862, his son died and he got extremely empathetic and he started even turning to God and praying like he never had before. Historians have called it a "Damascus Road" experience for him. Then he just said come hell or high water, I'm doing this. No one in his cabinet really wanted him to, and he said I'm doing it.

He changed the course of the war, and he changed the course of history. By making the war about human freedom, liberating the captive, and then the whole thing changed, which lead to the 13th amendment and so forth.

This is what we all need to do: Stop putting the walls up. These are real kids and they don't have anybody, and if we don't open up, no one's going to open up. But, when you do open up, it hurts a little bit. Then you become so much more effective in what you're trying to do. Ideas and inspiration, I'd argue even miracles, start happening when you do that."

NEWS REPORTER KATHRYN MAY:
Operation Underground Railroad is a fairly new
organization, just over two years old, but it's
captured a lot of media attention with its missions to
rescue child slaves throughout the world.

India. Haiti. Mexico. They go into the darkest corners
of the world and work with law enforcement to rescue
children from slavery. Since its inception a little
over two years ago, they've helped authorities arrest
over 157 people in 12 different countries.

KATHRYN MAY
@KATHRYNMAYKSL

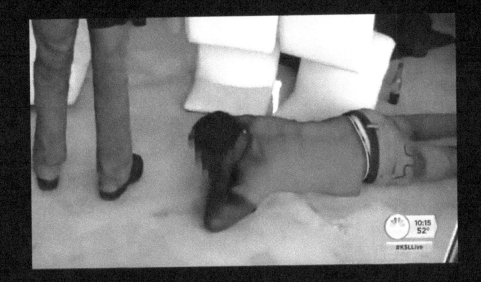

SCENE/LOCATION:
Operation Toussaint Briefing

TIM BALLARD:

I never dreamed that I would work in Haiti. I didn't know anything, really, about Haiti. Until I learned about a little boy who was born in Utah, a US citizen, who was kidnapped in Haiti from his church where his father was the pastor. That little boy was taken and he was kidnapped.

I read about it in the local newspaper and I just had to do something about it. I thought that I could make it into a US case, and I couldn't because it wasn't; it was a Haitian case. The man, the father of this boy, who I met, who changed my world, is Guesno Mardy. Guesno's sitting right here. Guesno, will you just stand up? This is Guesno Mardy and I have so much to say about Guesno.

We went to Haiti to look for his son, but the only way for us to go to Haiti would be to...we had to leave our jobs. I had to leave my job, because I didn't have enough leave from work.

SCENE/LOCATION:
Interview with Tim Ballard,
continues

TIM BALLARD:

I loved my job. I loved working for Homeland Security. It's, I mean, these are the best people on the planet doing the best work, and all the colleagues I had floated this idea to before, in the weeks leading up…said, "You're crazy. Don't do this. You're crazy."

John Lines looked at me and he started off with, "You're crazy." And I'm like, here we go again, you know, but he said something different...he said, "You're crazy if you don't try this."

SCENE/LOCATION:
Interview with Jonathan Lines,
continues

JONATHAN LINES:

I was encouraging, overtly; but in my heart of hearts I thought, that's going to be a tough go. That's going to be a tough go to leave the security of the US government and go save children around the world.

SCENE/LOCATION:
Interview with Tim Ballard,
continues

TIM BALLARD:

Three years old. Gardy. His name was Gardy. They kidnapped him from the church where Guesno was the pastor. They took him, this little boy, and they trafficked him. This happens all the time in Haiti.

"I remember reading the story and I…there was a picture of Guesno and my heart just melted. As a father, it just melted for him. I know, I have enough experience to know, very little is being done to find this little boy."

Guesno Mardy

SCENE/LOCATION:
Interview with Guesno Mardy

GUESNO MARDY:
He was three when they took
him and now he's 10. When that
first happened, I couldn't
sleep at night. I couldn't
even get into my house and
sleep, because as a father,
my job is getting my son back.
I spent months before I could
even get into the house and
sleep inside.

One of the suspects, I knew
him. Usually, I don't know
for everywhere, but in Haiti,
people who kidnap others...
they don't do that randomly.
They know the victims, you
know. Even when the legal
authorities say there's
nothing that they can do
about it... One of the times

I talked to them, they asked
me to bring them a solid lead.
They will come and destroy
whatever to get him back to
me, but I have to get the
lead. I have no means for
doing that.

Sometimes when people are on
holidays, I took my vehicle
and went into the mountains
trying to—in a public, open
market—trying to see if my boy
might come there. It's a very
long trip.

I feel that it is my duty.
It is my responsibility to
get him back. And I will
not let go.

SCENE/LOCATION:
Operation Toussiant Briefing

TIM BALLARD:

We got to Haiti, and we worked with law enforcement and we went in there looking for Gardy. We never found him. What we did find was two things: we found that this child was trafficked through what looked to be an orphanage. It wasn't an orphanage, and we were asked by the Haitian police to go undercover with hidden cameras and go into this place that was selling children. They were selling children for $10,000 and then they raised the price to $15,000.

The traffickers were selling kids and we were able to dismantle that organization and we had to buy two children in the process. We had to buy two children and they were the key to getting the other kids out.

After we got those kids out, and his son was not there, I said Guesno, "I'm so sorry. Your son's not there."

There was 28 children that were rescued, but his son was not there. I started to cry and Guesno was crying, but he only cried for a little bit and then he popped his head up and he said, "Don't you realize what just happened?"

And I said, "What? What just happened?"

He's smiling now, and I don't know why he's smiling—cause he's a very smiley guy, and he has a light about him. I learned what that light was, because he said, "If Gardy had never been kidnapped, then your team never would've come here. These 28 kids would be for sale or be sold."

I said, "Yeah, I guess I never thought of it that way."

Then he said maybe the most profound thing that anyone has ever said to me, he said, "If I have to sacrifice my son so that these 28 kids can be rescued, that's a sacrifice I'm willing to make."

That's when I knew that we would never leave Haiti, because of the spirit of that Haitian man. Who then, by the way, went to the police station the next day and he said, "I will take home any of those children that were rescued in the name of my son. I will take them home."

He took eight of those children home that day, and he is their father today in Haiti. So, you see, we could never leave Haiti after that. We decided we had to do more operations. We had to dig deeper and look for Gardy. Dig deeper.

SCENE/LOCATION:
Interview with Tim Ballard, continues

TIM BALLARD:

The more we go looking for Gardy, a funny thing happens. Every time we look for him, we find other kids.

TIM BALLARD:

"Gardy is the kid whose story created Operation Underground Railroad."

Photo of Gardy

What's in the video?

He's got a 14 year old right here.
-Yea, 14 in the video.

Have you (expletive) the girl too?

SCENE/LOCATION:
Operation Toussiant Briefing

TIM BALLARD:

I sat across from these guys as they told me about the children that they had been raping. They laughed about it; they laughed and they scoffed. They said, "You get to do it next," and it's horrifying. Horrifying.

Now, this was on super bowl Sunday and this is where the story gets very interesting...

SCENE/LOCATION:
News clip

NEWSCASTER:

Super Bowl Sunday, a lot of Americans have a little Super Bowl Party, hot wings and watching the big game. But a local non-profit organization that fights human trafficking spent their super bowl weekend in Haiti.

SCENE/LOCATION:
Haiti, Super Bowl Sunday, 2017

TIM BALLARD:

Will you take the 11 year old? Your youngest?

SCENE/LOCATION:
News clip

NEWSCASTER:

Timothy Ballard and his team at Operation Underground Railroad worked undercover pretending to purchase young girls for sex. Ballard says the men sold him 20 minors, as young as 11 years old.

SCENE/LOCATION:
Interview with Jessica Mass

JESSICA MASS
Director of Aftercare, O.U.R.:

"It was super bowl Sunday, February 5th, 2017, we had set up this operation that looked like it went flawless."

SCENE/LOCATION:
Operation Toussiant Briefing

MATT OSBORNE
Former C.I.A Operative, SVP
O.U.R. Rescue & Recovery:

In Operation Underground Railroad
we always want to ensure that if these
rescued children cannot go back to their
parents, then they go into vetted safe
houses, orphanages, or rehabilitation
centers. Our aftercare team, lead by Ms.
Jessica Mass, who is here with us today,
spent weeks liasioning with partners
in Haiti. Not just Guesno and his safe
house, but others whose names cannot
be shared now for their own protection.

SCENE/LOCATION:
Interview with Tim Ballard, continues

TIM BALLARD:

We'll go into a country and the first question we ask, if the police or that government wants to work with us, is what kind of aftercare capabilities are you aware of? These kids, so many of them, there isn't a home to go home to.

It's not like this happy story all the time, where it's like, "Oh your loving family has been waiting for you in the garden and the trees are there and the beautiful flowers, and just go hug them and all is well."

I mean there's…generally that's not the case. I wish it were, but generally the fact is there was no family, or the family was part of the problem. That's how they got trafficked.

SCENE/LOCATION:
Interview with Glenn Beck, continues:

GLENN BECK:

That's where everybody else screws it up. It's where we screwed up. That's the reconstruction part. The ending of the slavery was good. Now, how do we make sure that we provide the tools [these kids need] to be able to make it and be able to have a fair shot at something they've never experienced before? I can't even imagine the scarring that they have. And to be able to see them turn their lives around, remarkable.

CASE NAME	OBJECTIVE	STATUS
Operation Toussaint	Operation Underground Railroad and the Fight to End Modern Day Slavery	Ongoing

SCENE/LOCATION:
Operation Toussiant Briefing

MATT OSBORNE:

We laid out the whole operation. You saw from the video, the beautiful Kaliko Beach Club.

TIM BALLARD:

We have to play the role of very wealthy sex tourists, and so we had the whole operation set up. It went beautifully.

SCENE/LOCATION:
News Clip

NEWSCASTER:

When police arrived they arrested nine men from three separate human trafficking rings and liberated 29 victims.

SCENE/LOCATION:
Operation Toussiant Briefing

MATT OSBORNE:

Our Haitian partners did an amazing job. We made the arrest, and we got the girls immediately to the area where we were assured that they would get the support they need.

SCENE/LOCATION:
Interview with Jessica Mass

JESSICA MASS:

We were so excited. We were excited that these girls were finally going to have hope and healing. It was just a couple days after, that I received a phone call.

SCENE/LOCATION:
Operation Toussiant Briefing

MATT OSBORNE:

We unfortunately got some very frustrating news a few days after the operation.

SCENE/LOCATION:
Interview with Jessica Mass

JESSICA MASS:

The traffickers were being released and all the girls were released.

SCENE/LOCATION:
Operation Toussiant Briefing

TIM BALLARD:

They get released. They get freed. They pay money to the right people; to the judges. I remember when we got that word, I remember Jessica, Matt....we were in tears. We were in tears. We couldn't believe that these kids could be put in harm's way again.

SCENE/LOCATION:
Interview with Jessica Mass

JESSICA MASS:

Half the girls had family members that showed up, and the other half had traffickers that showed up for them.

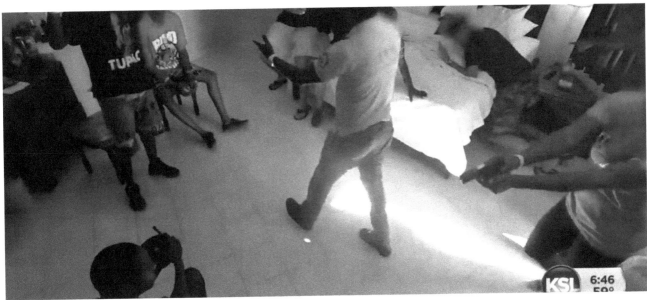

SCENE/LOCATION:
Operation Toussiant Briefing

TIM BALLARD:

These guys who were laughing about raping children were now laughing their way home.

We didn't know what to do. We had some long talks about it and with Guesno and Demitri and they just said please don't give up. Don't give up. There are good people in this government that want this problem to go away.

And what happened was what we hoped would happen. The good people who didn't know what happened to us, they came to us. The good people came to us and they said, we didn't know this truth. We didn't know what happened, but we will not stand for it.

And I'm looking at the good people right now, who came to us. The job's not quite done, but it's almost done, because now we need to go back and we need to re-arrest every single one of these traffickers.

It will be a message to Haiti, to America, to the whole world that there are good people everywhere that will stand up for this. That there is light in this dark world. There's light. If we don't become that light, there is no light.

ATTORNEY GENERAL OCNAM:

(Speaking through a translator) I was listening to your words. I should be the one to thank you guys, because you choose to come help me and my country. When I became attorney general, I saw that case in my office. I saw that case about the trafficking in Kaliko Beach.

First, what I said, "I'm going to fire all the judges." Second, I am going to go and get the other people. I met the President of Haiti, Jovenel Moise. I tell them, "If they don't want me to do this work, I'm not going to work anymore."

The first part was to fire those judges. And I've done this. Sometimes they try to threaten me over the telephone, but I'm not scared. Because I want to keep going with this cause. Instead of telling me thank you, I will be working together with you to keep working. And we are going to fight.

PORT-AU-PRINCE
HAITI

Operation Toussaint
January 2018

O.U.R Operational Briefing
January 2018

DAVE LOPEZ
Jump Team Lead/ Ex-Navy Seal:

We finally have our eyes on what's going on.
We're shifting our mindset. There are two of
them that we still need to verify, and we're
going to have reconnaissance teams running
the rest of the day. It limits what we want
to do during the day. We would rather not do
a snatch and grab on the side of the street
in the daytime. It's very hard to sneak up to
people the way this traffic is, and do that
effectively. It's very low chance; I'm talking
like a 15% chance of getting these guys.

Just so everyone knows, Andrew knows this area
we're going to better than anyone. He's lived
there for periods of his life, so he knows
this better...honestly, he knows this better
than the police that are putting us in there.
He knows this area.

ANDREW
Recon Specialist/ Translator:

In a nutshell, top of the trees perspective,
our activities tonight are going to take place
in Pétion-Ville, which is a wealthier part of
Port-Au-Prince where there are several hotels.
So there's a lot of working, there's a lot of
prostitution going on. That's where…

TIM BALLARD:

Wealthier being a very relative term.

ANDREW:

(Nodding) For Haiti. It's a place where
foreigners come. So if you're a foreigner,
you're going to come here. You're going
to stay most likely in Pétion-Ville, so
that's what attracts some of the nefarious
activities.

DAVE LOPEZ:

So any questions about the area? We're going
to pull up Google Maps, we've dropped pins on
everything. So everyone's going to get a good
visual of the area that we're looking at.

Jump Team Lead /
Ex-Navy Seal
Dave Lopez

Recon Specialist / Translator
Andrew

SCENE/LOCATION:
In the van doing reconnaissance

DIMITRI
Local Ground Recon/ Private Investigator:

Okay guys, as we do this, tinted windows, and
out there, I seen lights out there, there
shouldn't be lights back there.

DAVE LOPEZ:

No, they need to turn those off.

DIMITRI:

Okay, we are in an unmarked van. It's a van
that is used for taxis. In a few minutes, I'm
going to have to put my windows down, because
it's not known to have taxis, you know, having
their windows up freezing.

DAVE LOPEZ:
I understand.

SCENE/LOCATION:
Operation Toussaint, January 2018 - O.U.R.
Operational Briefing

DAVE LOPEZ:
In a nutshell, the bird's eye view here is we're
going after three different targets and one of
them is a female. This is our ace in the hole
mission. If everything else fails, we're getting
this chick tonight. She's awful. Andrew can go
into more detail.

SCENE/LOCATION:
In the van doing reconnaissance

ANDREW:
Is Cho (female trafficker), is she going to be
out on the street? Is she like a pimp and has
some prostitutes working for her? Do you know
what we're going to be looking for?

DIMITRI:
Yeah, she's into trafficking, and she's a
boss. She's the head of a cartel. Okay, she's
like a captain. A captain in a mafia.

SCENE/LOCATION:
Operation Toussaint, January 2018 - O.U.R.
Operational Briefing

ANDREW:
Our hotel's right here: Best Western in
Pétion-Ville. She's literally, like, two
blocks away and one down, typically. But she
kind of moves within, I would say, a one
block radius of that spot.

SCENE/LOCATION:
In the van doing reconnaissance

DIMITRI:
She's crossing the street. She's crossing
the street. That's Cho right there. Crossing
the street with the white pants. That's her
right there. That's Cho right there. That's
the boss right there.

ANDREW:
We have eyes on her. She does not like this.

DIMITRI:
That's the boss right there.

ANDREW:
All those girls are working for her. She's
their pimp, and Cho is number one. She pimps
out young girls. She has the legal girls on
the street, visible, but she has a little
house back there where one of our operators
has seen underage girls.

NICK NANTON
Documentary Director:
He just got behind us.

DAVE LOPEZ:
He just came behind us? Just pay attention
to it.

DAVE LOPEZ:
Hey Dimitri, it's possible we a tail. It's
possible we have a tail behind us.

DIMITRI:
Okay.

NICK NANTON:
Wait never mind, he's turning off. We're
good.

SCENE/LOCATION:
Operation Toussaint, January 2018 - O.U.R.
Operational Briefing

DAVE LOPEZ:
If there are any holes in the logic right
now, anything glaring that anyone is thinking
about, this is the time to beat it to death.
Because this is all coming together very
quick, and I guarantee there's more things.

TIM BALLARD:
You know what I want to do is, start with a
prayer. What about your special prayer?

DAVE LOPEZ:
Want me to pray that prayer? Alright, let's
bow our heads and I'll sing it real quick.

(Sings prayer in Hebrew, then repeats the
prayer in English)

"May Yehovah bless you and
keep you. May Yehovah let his
face shine upon on you and be
gracious to you. May Yehovah
lift up his countenance upon you
and give you shalom. Amen."

ENTIRE GROUP:
Amen

O.U.R / Haitian Operative Training

O.U.R. / Haitian
Operative Training

Jump team briefing,
20 minutes to launch

Jump Team Briefing
20 minutes to launch

MEDIC:

Okay, this is the part that nobody really
wants to talk about or do, but that's the
part we probably need to know the best, if
somebody gets shot or stabbed or severely
injured enough that they have to be taken to
a higher level of care. We've got a number of
these kits that are going to be spread out in
the vehicles. These are what we call blow out
kits, so ... Is anybody in here familiar with
medicine besides the medic...

[NO ONE RESPONDS]

MEDIC:

Okay, so then none of this stuff is going
to matter to you. However, at that time if
somebody gets hurt and somebody yells medic,
everything else needs to stop. Nothing else
matters, because you could lose a person at
that point, right? So, the Haitians are going
to do whatever they're going to do, but this
group in here, we're going to keep that person
alive.

DAVE LOPEZ:

Our target's name is Cho. She is a pimp who
is going to be on the street corner about two
or three blocks from here. We intend to take
Cho and try and use her to get information.
We've got eight other targets that are out
there that were stupidly released. We know
that she paid $80,000 to someone to get out
of jail. We really want to understand where
she got $80,000 from. We believe a criminal
organization supports her. We've been to her
house. She's not living large at all, so if
she's backed by someone, we want to find out,
"Who paid you the $80,000, and who within the
government did you give that $80,000 to?"

In addition, we want to just scare the living
daylights out of her and use the momentum and,
kind of, fear. Saying, "Just, listen, the
next five minutes of your life are going to
determine the next fifty years of your life."

This is our plan. Once the Haitians come,
we'll-

TM BALLARD:
It's their country, of course. So we do what
they want.

ANDREW:
Right.

DAVE LOPEZ:
Perimeter 1 and Perimeter 2, as long as we've
got eyes looking outboard with guns while
we're in the middle, that's the only goal
here. We're making these things really simple.
Look, we don't all rush to the middle of the
action. That's what rookies do, right? That's
what idiots do. They have a job, and even if
they don't like their job, even if it's not
the cool job, this is their damn job.

ANDREW:
I think it goes without saying, we don't want
them to know where we're staying tonight at
all, and if we need to take different routes…
or just be really familiar with who is behind
you and who could be following you, even if
it's a little motorcycle. Those guys are the
worst. Motorcycle guys are bad, and they're
going to be informants. We want to sleep
safely, and those driving to the airport
tomorrow, we don't want any issues.

PÉTION-VILLE POLICE CHIEF:
  Hey, guys.

TIM BALLARD:
  Are the guys downstairs?

JIM:
  We have 17 guys all together from my side.

TIM BALLARD:
  Perfect. The Recon-1, we're like three minutes
  to deploying.

JIM:
  Okay, driver's down there. He's waiting.

Petion-Ville
Police Chief

We have 17 guys
all together from my side.

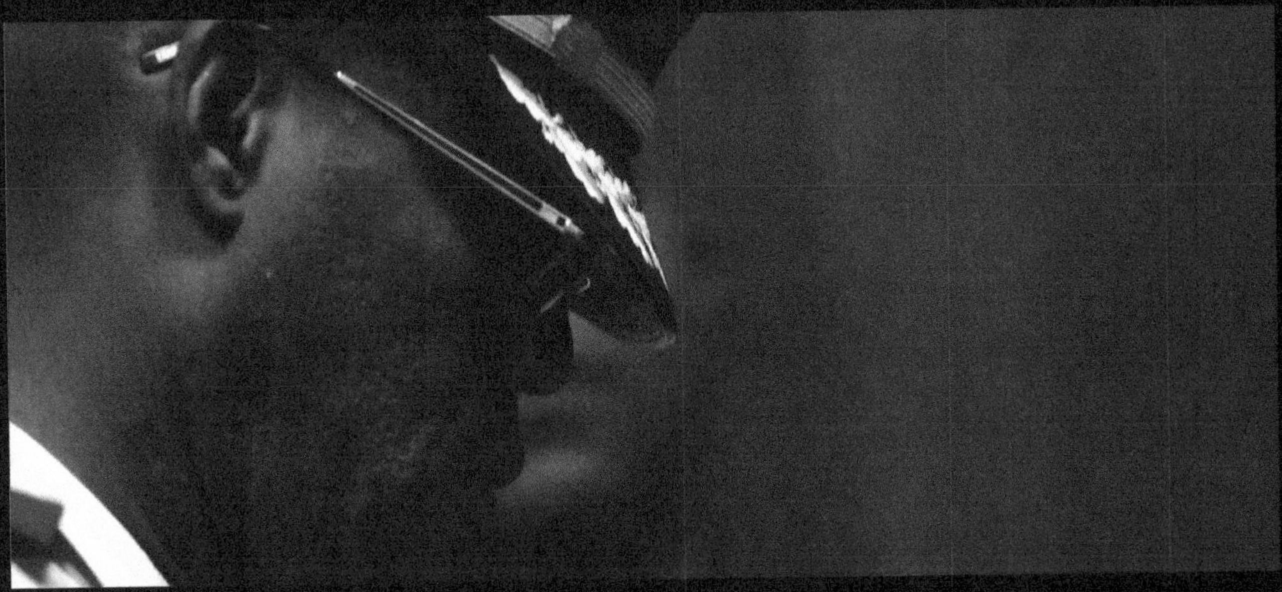

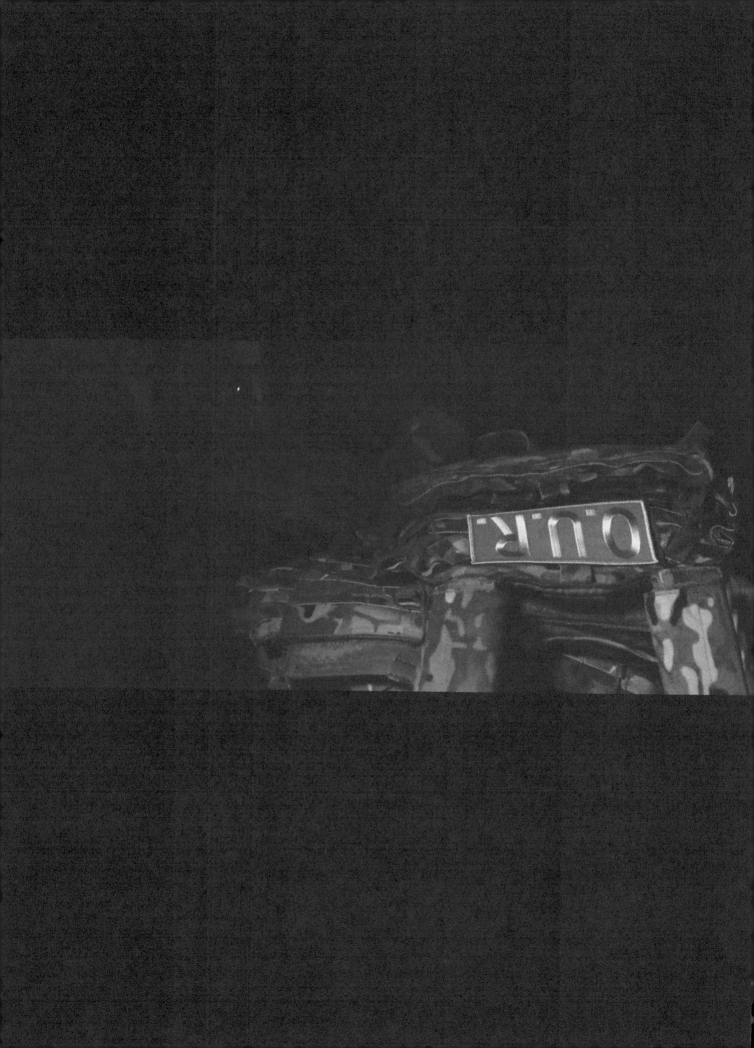

SCENE/LOCATION:
In the van on the way to the mission

ANDREW:
  {Prayer in Haitian Creole}

ANDREW:
  All right you guys. Up there, where the lights
  are, is about where she's at. It's this car
  pulled over.

TIM BALLARD:
  Are we close, man?

ANDREW:
  Yeah, it's right here. Ready?

ALL IN CAR:
  Un. Deux. Trois! Go! Go! Go! Go! Go!

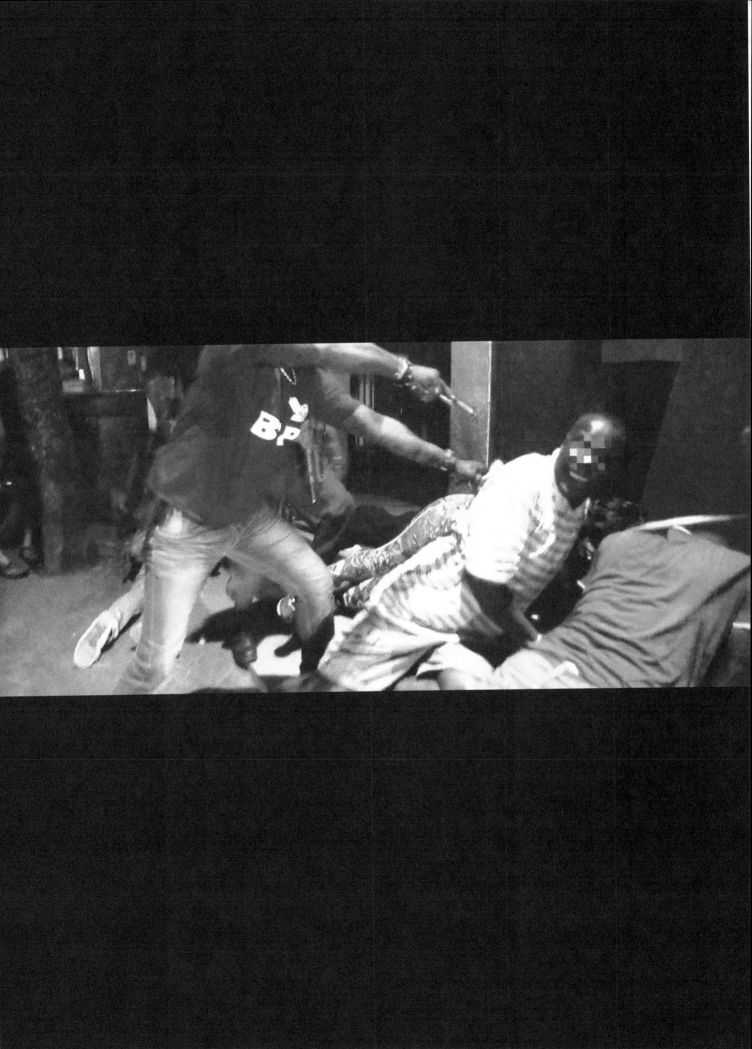

Go in front and block them.

We'll become that perimeter.

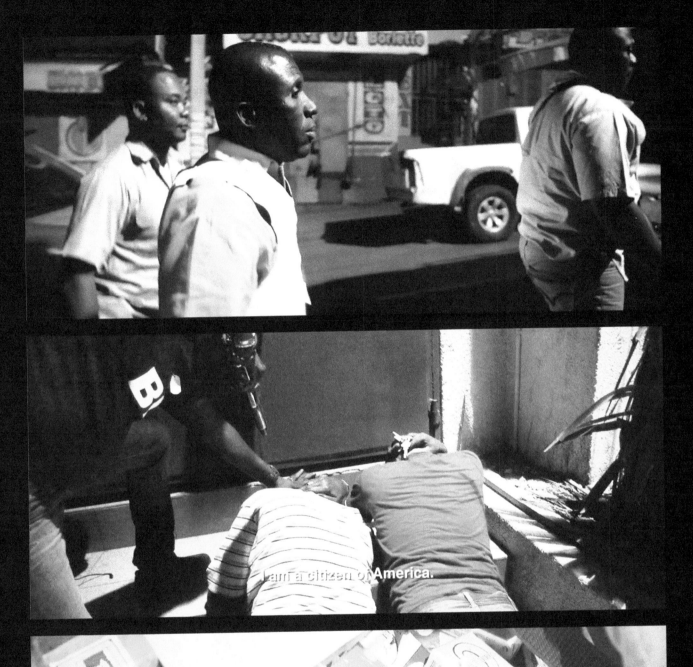

"Cho's" Brothel

During the raid,
this undercover camera caught a pedophile raping a minor.

This is tragic and graphic, and will only be
used as evidence to prosecute this case.

DIMITRI: Who did you pay to get out of jail?

CHO: I'm not going to lie.
I don't know these words.

CHO: I'm not going to say.
Im not going to rat on no one!

That lady, she's the one
that got arrested already?

-At Kaliko Bay?

SEAN REYES:
Thank you.
You're an inspiration to all of us.

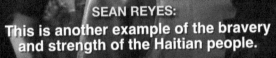

SEAN REYES:
**This is another example of the bravery
and strength of the Haitian people.**

ATTORNEY GENERAL OCNAM:
**What's important for me is
we made this effort and we made this happen.**

ATTORNEY GENERAL OCNAM:
With a lot of preparation and work.

ATTORNEY GENERAL OCNAM:
And I am prepared to collaborate
with you so we can keep up this work...

ATTORNEY GENERAL OCNAM:
so there's zero human trafficking.

SCENE/LOCATION:
Interview with Tim, continues

TIM BALLARD:

We get the kids out; four kids are pulled out of these dens of nightmares and they're in our safe house. Jessica Mass, our director of after care is with them, and they start to open up. They start to talk, and the one little girl, the youngest of them, starts to cry. She starts to tear up and she said, "This is the first time that I've ever felt hope, that I can remember."

She preceded to tell us this story about how when she was about six or seven years old, she was kidnapped in the wake of the earthquake. Her parents were killed in the earthquake, like so many parents were, and she was left an orphan instantly. This nice woman comes up, tells her that she'll take care of her, and to come with her.

This was happening all over in the wake of the earthquake. In the case of Rosie, she was six or seven years old. Cho gets ahold of her, promises to take care of her, and instead puts her into a life of sex slavery. This was so crazy, she said, "It's amazing that you guys came and rescued me on January 12. It was January 12, eight years ago, when the earthquake struck."

SCENE/LOCATION:
At an aftercare center

TIM BALLARD:

Hey hey, hey buddy. How are you?

SCENE/LOCATION:
Interview with Tim, continues

TIM BALLARD:

This little girl was in the most obscure country in the world. Not only that, she was in the most obscure, darkest corner of that most obscure country just wallowing in hell; far from anyone who, possibly, could care.

SCENE/LOCATION:
At an aftercare center

TIM BALLARD:

You're so big!

SCENE/LOCATION:
Interview with Tim, continues

TIM BALLARD:

It took her 24 hours after the rescue to even talk, because she said she couldn't believe anyone would come for her.

SCENE/LOCATION:
At an aftercare center

TIM BALLARD:

Santa Claus? Who is that?

COLEEN:

Santa Claus.

TIM BALLARD:

Santa Claus? He came? Santa Claus came here?

SCENE/LOCATION:
Interview with Tim, continues

TIM BALLARD:

It's what we are trying to do. We intentionally go to the darkest corners of the Earth where there is no hope and find these kids. What that does, apart from liberating children, what that does is it provides hope for everybody now.

Where there was no hope, there's hope everywhere. If we can continue to grow our operations and continue to get the support we need, there is hope everywhere for the first time.

FILE NO 146

FILE NO. 149

My name is Coleen...

Coleen Jean-Baptist Catel Ballard.

Cole Jean-Baptist Ballard.

SCENE/LOCATION:
Operation Toussaint Briefing

TIM BALLARD:

(Speaking about Operation Voo Doo Doll, 2014) We did find two things. We found them trafficking and selling kids and we were able to dismantle that organization. We had to buy two children in the process. We had to buy two children; and they were the key to getting the other kids out. We've told that story many times, but what's special about those two children is that I've formed a special bond with them.

When we were driving from the orphanage to the sting house in the hotel, this little boy jumped up into my lap, and I'm supposed to be this, you know, hard criminal. After the rescue was done, my wife and I couldn't stop thinking about them, him and his sister, they were the two kids. So we started to work toward adopting them. That was almost four years ago and I just got the email today, the decree came out of Parquet, and their names are now Ballard. They're my children.

If I lived in Haiti, I could take them home right now. All we have to wait for now are passports and visas and then they can come home to Utah.

SCENE/LOCATION:
At Tim Ballard's family home in Utah

TIM BALLARD:

Where's Cole and Coleen going to sleep

DELLA, TIM'S DAUGHTER:

I don't know.

TIM BALLARD:

We have one extra bedroom, right?

DELLA:

Yeah, but where's Daniel going to sleep?

TIM BALLARD:

He's gonna bunk with the boys.

LUKE, TIM'S SON:

He's going to sleep with me.

TIM BALLARD:

With Luke.

LUKE:

Yes!

TIM'S WIFE, KATHERINE:

There are days that Tim and I are like, "What? Why do we have all these kids?" It just...you look at this little guy, and he is so loved, and by just by virtue of the fact that he was born in a family and that automatically gives him access to this love that we don't even have to think about. It's just there.

There are so many children around the world that don't have that, and that could. There just shouldn't be this much excess with that many children in need.

As of 2018, Operation Underground Railroad has rescued 1,000
victims and assisted in the arrests of 443 traffickers
around the world.

Gardy Mardy is still missing.

"I'll find him. It is something
that I don't have to talk about
because I know I will find him. I
will find him. One day something
will happen. I'll find him."

Guesno

A special thank you for their involvement and
contributions to this project goes out to the
following people and organizations:

MyMedic
Operation Underground Railroad
The Ballard Family
Department of Homeland Security
The Abolitionists
Loop Haiti
Tony Robbins
Axiom Images
Pond 5
WXYZ Detroit
RTV 6

NEED A KEYNOTE SPEAKER FOR YOUR EVENT?

We have thousands of Best-Selling Authors® and Experts ready to share with your audience!

Contact Impact Speakers Group today, we'd love to help!

ImpactSpeakersGroup.com

iMPACT | Speakers Group

CPSIA information can be obtained
at www.ICGtesting.com
Printed in the USA
BVHW090338110620
581248BV00004B/11